St. Godric

An Eggsplorers Story

First published by the North East Religious
Learning Resources Centre, 2022

www.resourcescentreonline.co.uk

eggsplorers@gmail.com

St. Godric

An Eggsplorers Story

Written & Illustrated

by

Sue Tinker

Godric's mother and father taught him to love God when he was a little boy.

Godric wanted to be a sailor
when he grew up.

Godric sailed to exciting places. He and his mother visited the Holy Land where Jesus had lived.

It was hot and tiring. Godric carried his mother when she was too tired to walk. They believed that an angel was watching over and helping them.

Godric went to visit the island of Lindisfarne. When he was there he believed he had seen St. Cuthbert who told him how he should live his life for God.

Godric gave away all that
he owned and went to live
in a cave to be alone and
worship God.

He wore heavy armour to remind himself to concentrate on God.

Godric's life was hard and he was
tempted to do the wrong thing many
times, to make his life easier
.....but he fought the temptation.

People brought him food and
he shared what he had with the
creatures of the forest.

22

Godric made up and sang songs
to praise God.
He believed that Mary the mother
of Jesus had visited him and taught
him to sing a song of praise.

Battles were fought close to Godric's cave but God kept him safe.
To say thank you he built a chapel where people could worship.

When Godric became old and frail the monks from Durham cared for him. Instead of his animal hair shirt they gave him one of their black habits to wear.

When Godric died the monks took his
chainmail tunic. They unpicked all the
the metal rings.
These rings were thought to have
 special holy powers because Godric was
 such a holy man. The rings were used
                    to help people.

Author and illustrator Sue Tinker is also the creator of the Bible Eggsplorers. Eggsplorers are hardy, durable, hand-sized resources designed to teach children about core stories from scripture, including those from Christianity, Judaism, Hinduism and more! With her support, the Religious Resources Centre has created a St Godric Eggsplorer set which can be borrowed for school or church use with children aged between 2 and 12.

You can borrow this, and all of the Eggsplorers sets, from the North East Religious Learning Resources Centre: www.resourcescentreonline.co.uk. There are more Godric-related materials, including some designed for parents and teachers, on the same website.

You can also contact Sue Tinker: eggsplorers@gmail.com

Finchale, near Durham City in the North East of England, still contains archaeological evidence of the Christian communities that have lived and worshipped in this area over many hundreds of years. Whilst nothing remains of St Godric's hermitage, you can still visit and explore this significant historic site today. Finchale is also a stop on the English Camino: a developing pilgrimage route that links Finchale and Durham to Santiago in Spain, where Godric himself went on pilgrimage.

https://britishpilgrimage.org/portfolio/finchale-camino-ingles

Photograph by Simon Webb

Also published by the Religious Resources Centre

Long ago, in a kingdom by the sea, there was a Golden Age. This sounds like something from a fairy tale, but these are true stories of the men and women who brought light to the north of England. There was Oswald, who against all odds saved his people from tyranny. Aidan and Cuthbert carried God's love across the kingdom. Hilda set up a community where scholars and cowherds found their voices. You can meet them, and some others like them, here.

Northern Saints by Margaret McAllister, illustrated by Amy Warmington.
Full colour throughout; also available as an e-book. ISBN 978-1791528652

enquiries@resourcescentreonline.co.uk

Printed in Great Britain
by Amazon

80258667R00020